# All About Chocolate

## Madison Spielman

# Table of Contents

# Chocolate Dreams

Close your eyes and imagine your favorite chocolate candy. Think about how it smells. Think about the taste. Think how it melts in your mouth.

# Mmmmm! Are you ready for some chocolate now?

If you are like most people in the United States, you love chocolate, and you eat about twelve pounds of it each year!

# The First Chocolate

cacao beans

Chocolate started out a very long time ago as a type of drink made in South America. But hard chocolate that people can eat was not made until much later.

cacao pod

People long ago did not have chocolate. Chocolate like we have today was not made until 1828.

In that year, a Dutch chemist removed the cocoa butter from cocoa beans. Cocoa butter tastes bitter.

Without the cocoa butter, cocoa powder was left. Cocoa powder is the delicious beginning of chocolate.

A DISPENSER.

You can see where England and Switzerland are on the map on pages 12 and 13.

FRY'S CHOCOLATE
90 PRIZE MEDALS
MAKERS TO THE QUEEN

The first solid chocolate was sold in England in 1847.

In 1875, a Swiss man added milk to chocolate and made the first milk chocolate. That is the kind of chocolate in most candy today.

# Where Does Chocolate Come From?

Chocolate is made from the seeds of the **cacao** tree. The seeds grow inside pods. They are called cocoa beans.

Cacao (kuh-KAY-oh) comes from the Latin word that means "food of the gods."

They should really be called cacao beans. But long ago, English speaking people spelled cacao wrong by mistake. People have just kept it that way.

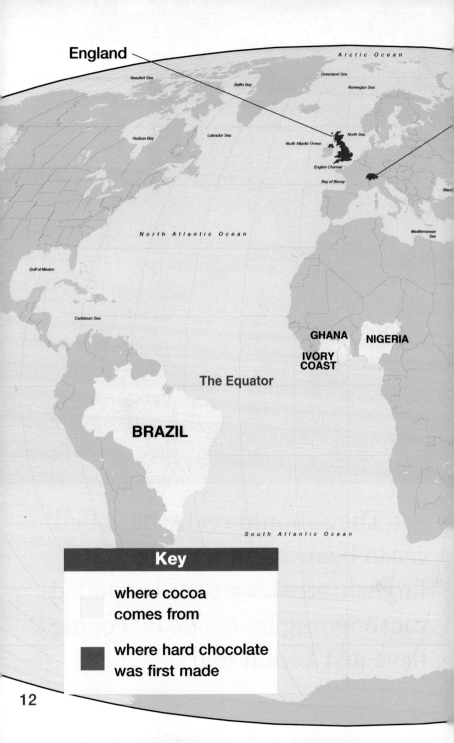

England

Arctic Ocean

Beaufort Sea

Greenland Sea

Baffin Bay

Norwegian Sea

Hudson Bay

Labrador Sea

North Sea

North Atlantic Ocean

English Channel

Bay of Biscay

North Atlantic Ocean

Black

Mediterranean Sea

Gulf of Mexico

Caribbean Sea

GHANA

NIGERIA

IVORY COAST

The Equator

BRAZIL

South Atlantic Ocean

## Key

where cocoa comes from

where hard chocolate was first made

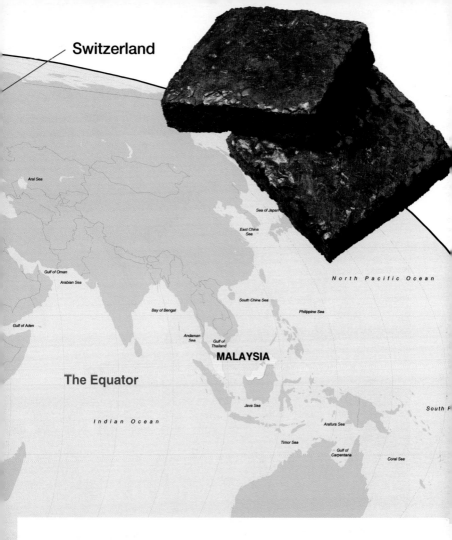

Switzerland

Aral Sea

Sea of Japan

East China
Sea

Gulf of Oman

Arabian Sea

North Pacific Ocean

South China Sea

Bay of Bengal

Philippine Sea

Andaman
Sea

Gulf of
Thailand

**MALAYSIA**

**The Equator**

Java Sea

South P

Indian Ocean

Arafura Sea

Gulf of Aden

Timor Sea

Gulf of
Carpentaria

Coral Sea

Most of the world's cocoa
beans come from countries in
South America, Africa, and Asia.
Look at the map to find them.

# How Is Chocolate Made?

It takes time and work to make good chocolate.

Ferment means to change slowly. Yeast and bacteria can cause this chemical change.

First, the cacao pods must be picked. Then they are **fermented** for six days.

When they are ready, the pods are split open. The seeds are removed and dried.

They are dried in the sun for about seven days. Sometimes they are dried in special machines instead.

Next, the dried beans are sent to chocolate factories.

There the cocoa butter is removed, and the seeds are roasted and ground into powder.

The powder is mixed with sugar, milk, or other ingredients to make different kinds of chocolate.

Next, the chocolate is heated in a special machine called a **conche**. The best chocolate is heated there for at least one week.

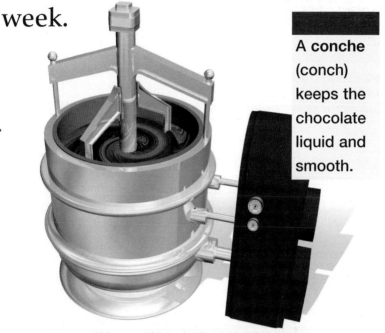

A **conche** (conch) keeps the chocolate liquid and smooth.

Finally, the chocolate is cooled slowly, warmed again, and cooled to its final hardness. Now, it is ready to be packaged and sent to stores where you can buy and eat it!

# Who Loves Chocolate?

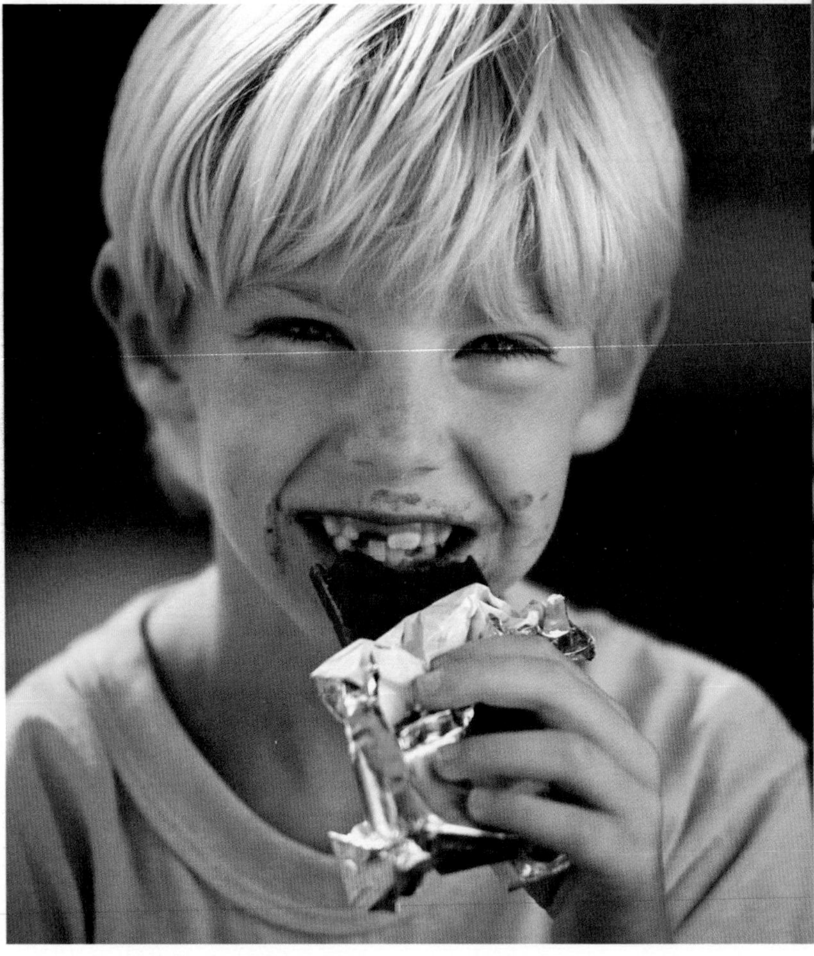

People in the United States eat almost half of all the chocolate eaten in the world.

But it is the Swiss people who love it best. The average person there eats twenty-two pounds of chocolate each year!

In fact, many people think that Swiss chocolate is the best chocolate in the world.

# Chocolate, Chocolate Everywhere!

Is chocolate only in candies? No! You can find chocolate in many different foods. Chocolate cake, pudding, cookies, ice cream, and hot cocoa are just a few of them. Wherever you find food, you can probably find some kind of chocolate, too.

What is your favorite chocolate food?

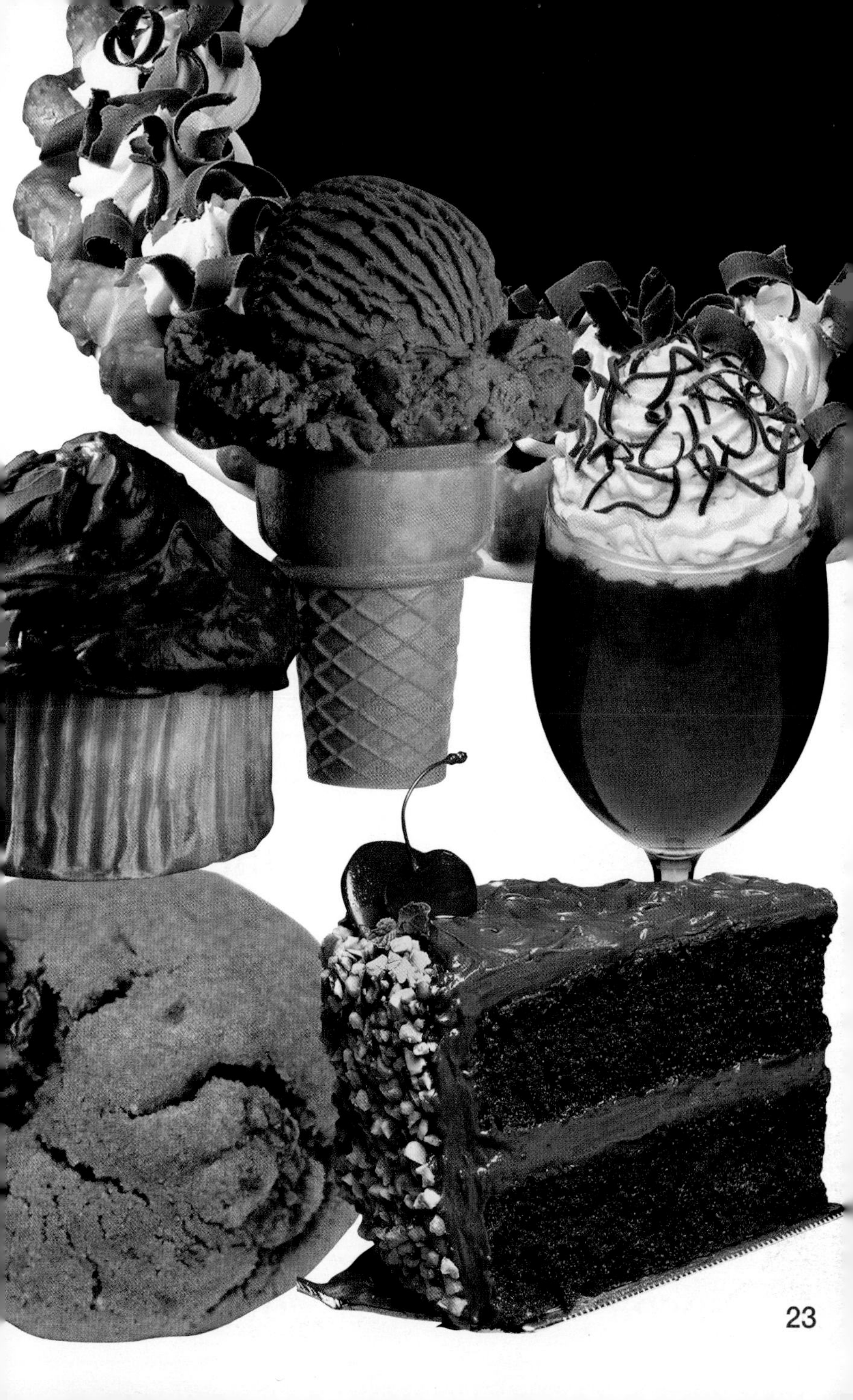

# Glossary

cacao beans

cacao pod

cacao tree

candies

cocoa powder

conche